Ordering:
A Season in My Garden

Poems by
Kenneth Pobo

Higganum Hill Books

First Edition
First Printing, September 15, 2001

Higganum Hill Books
P.O. Box 666   Higganum, Connecticut 06441-0666

Ph: (860) 345-4103
e-mail: rcdebold@connix.com

Library of Congress Control Number: 2001132582

ISBN: 0-9635185-5-0

Edited by Arthur S. Wensinger
Wesleyan University

Design by Mark G. Snyder
The Hartford Art School

Printed in the United States of America

CONTENTS

For Louis & Myrtle

I would like to thank the editors of the following magazines for publishing work from this collection: *Backspace, Black Dirt, Blue Unicorn, Buckle &, The Catbird Seat, Cedar Hill Review, Chaminade Review, Confrontation, Creeping Bent, Cumberland Poetry Review, Dharmacation, Empty, Expressive Spirals, The Fiddlehead, Forpoetry.Com, Galley Sail Review, Glass Cherry, Hanging Loose, Illuminations, Karamu, Kimera, Leapings, Libriumimplant, Mad Poets Review, The Magazine, Old Crow, One Trick Pony, Part-Time Postmodernist, Pavement Saw, Philadelphia Poets, Poetry Conspiracy, Poetry Down Under, Poetry Nottingham, Pulsar, River King Review, Riverwind, Roanoke Review, Secrets from the Orange Couch, Sidewalks, Sparks, Stagger, Thirteen, Tight, Various Artists, Western Ohio Review, Working Titles, Writers Round Table, and Yarrow.*

I.   DIG IN

"SPRING'S VOCIFEROUS GLORIES"
Tu Fu

The hate
language of fourteen-year-old
boys can't quite break
a ranunculus'
perfect
stillness. Cars

and motorcycles
vomit
exhaust. Even birds

act like big shots,
bossy in maples.
They could learn from
the silent worm
instead of eating him—

I almost yearn
for winter
when a snowflake
tiptoes on my roof
and plays
a white guitar.

HOW GARDENS WORK

I start my day touring
the garden. Morning
brings an unfolding leaf,
penstamon's sudden

ohmygod. I squint to see
only what the garden
cares to show me--most
of its real work
is in roots,
in a tenuous bargain
struck among soil, sun
and water. I go my way,

the top-secret network
of plants
with codes
we can never crack.

UP IT'S UP

Myrtle calls from Illinois
to say her allium giganteum's
already up--that's never
happened this early in
January before. In my
freezing flat, I've just
returned from the sauna
where I sweated out too
many taxis. Now Myrtle
bubbles up through phone
wires, full of flowers and
the amaze-us of spring.
My rooms smell of Mrs. Mullen's
cauliflower, but I have news
of an allium nudging winter's
icy snout close enough
to the sun to melt it.

GARDENING ADVICE

Expensive guidebooks say,
"Write everything down
so you'll remember what

you've ordered." True,
but I keep no records,
order one fantasy
after another all winter,
my mental garden roomier

than my real one. In May,
plants still arrive:
Balboa Blue Lizianthus.
Other Lizzies are cake
to find--with Balboa

I can explore an odder
variety. Where to put them?
My garden babbles
uneven leaves,
broken colors. I stick

a Lizzy here, a Lizzy there,
and hope. Next year,
again without clues,
my garden will be like the moon
if it escaped Earth's orbit,

happy to be free
but still trying to turn
our tides.

ON THE UP AND UP

up
up
    the first
  iris
    pushes
up
   Earth's
green
eyes
    almost hidden
     by dirt
till they
 rise
  high enough
   to watch
  winterfall
down

HELLEBORE SHOT

I scrunch down in mud
to shoot the round
red room of a hellebore

in bloom. Cold water
soaks into my crotch,
slides on my belly. Shivering,
I press myself deeper
into ooze. This flower

likes such slop. The picture
will remind me
of early spring
when I'm sitting indoors,
snow

falling,
the red blossom
worth the clammy sweetness
of leaky earth.

PAPERWHITES

Perhaps God
is paper and when

I die, all the paper
I've wasted
will find my name
on every crumple,
feel my breath
between the lines.

Paperwhites in
my window, delicate
as blank paper. Even
I would never
deface it
by attempting
a poem or letter,

yet I'm merciless
with the purity
of a tree
who gives her life
to make the paper

God who waits
for one good chance
to write on me

and crumple me
without a moment's
hesitation.

CREEPING CHARLEY

Creeping Charley does
one thing well--he creeps
and when he says,

"I've had enough creeping
for one day," he creeps

farther anyway. Flowers
loathe him--there's something
hoggy about him,

as if any spot of ground
ought to be his
alone. His attitude
makes me pull
and pull, much to the joy
 of rose and mullein.
A week later, he's crept

back, strong as ever,
the green noose of him
tightening around a stem.

DAFFODILS

right now
beautiful
models are locked
in underground
hotel rooms
they can't get out
with no
desire
to escape
they loll in the
luxury of lightless
evenings snow
often covering
each hotel
utterly until
spring when
they are ready
for work ready
to take root
and shoot up
perfect yellow
blossoms

JACK-IN-THE-PULPIT

Again this year,
Reverend Jack
has his back
to us--how can we

get his message
if he gives it
to a brick wall?
Is he making us
listen more closely
so his green

syllables don't get
carried away
by a wind
we rush after?

TROUBLED ANEMONES

I grew up hearing
how important it is
to get a head

start. I got one
and found my head
busted against a door.

I adjusted. My anemones
think that they need
a head start too, so

they tear through winter's
fence. When frost
fattens at night,

they look like parsley
that some busboy
scraped off a plate

while winter folds
his big hairy arms
and watches.

ARBORETUM IN APRIL

shoes muddy
jackets tied
around waists
we walk
sudden wind
a hand
on a bare chest
heartbeat under
index finger
dogs
trees shake
limbs loose
roots
deepen
sky drops
close around
our ears
a blue hat
grouchy earth
snarls
up violets

DOGWOOD AND REDBUD

Why not celebrate
spin of stamen—
a cabin with lights
shining between lid
and lash? Spring.
The dogwood
white and pink
as our most fragile
secret. Redbud,
slanted against
the mountain, spilling
from stone, asking us
into the future we share
with any rooted thing.
Our commercial hearts
reduced at Discount City
Flea Market - hidden
in a blossom net.
Trap me, quickly!
Don't let me out
till the last bloom
browns. By then
I will have become bark,
ark on the unseen
stream under your ankles.

MARTIN'S SPIDERWORT

In Tennessee
I wasn't happy
where pickups sport huge
Confederate flags,
where the Tennessee Volunteers
aren't a football team
but a religion, a lifestyle

choice. In Pennsylvania,
I miss creeping green kudzu,
the waltz of bud
and bud broken open. Spring
here is lusty and unbending,
but a far cry from Tennessee.

My friend Martin
from Knoxville mailed me
spiderwort roots—
it grows up looking like corn
till small blue cups

appear, six yellow dots
on the inside, cups
ample enough to hold
a Tennessee sky

hundreds of miles north,
sky that opens
along a tangle

of mountains, blue and
fierce at the edge of my eyes.

AMONG RHODODENDRONS

Among rhododendrons, your face
looks almost completely at peace.
Blossoms give you a kind of grace,
love, like you're ready to release

your spirit into a deep crease
of color. Can I follow you
where April's deep red buds increase,
where suburb becomes Xanadu?

I wonder if you're someone who
would rather travel alone, find
a flower without room for two.
What do I know? I'm often blind,

scared and confused. You settle me
down, build for me a hiding place.
We celebrate our mystery,
full blossoms of the commonplace.

CLEMATIS

The three clematis,
out at last! All
are magenta
against my gate.
How long they stayed
tight in swelling buds,
preparing for their debut--
in full bloom,
the sun's yellow lips
kiss them over and
over, the moon's mist
hands touch them
when we sleep.

WHAT LADYSLIPPERS DREAM

In the Wisconsin woods,
trees block out wind. It's still

where ferns romp, slip
and slide over moist pine
needles, autumn remnants.
We listen to birds rather
than talk about listening
to birds as we do back home.

We amble, letting trees
point the way. When a lake
comes into view, wind
picks up, ripples roll.
A pair of loons! How they
swim under water, hold
themselves down, bob up.

Or ladyslippers, dozens off
to the side. A dainty name,
yet they spring up
in bracken, stare bees down,
pink the forest floor. When

we die, let's come here again,
dream what ladyslippers dream.

II. WATCHING

THE WONDERFUL WORLD OF
GAZANIAS

By now they should be dead,
pushing up daisies,
as John Wayne might have said.

A Coke glass left out on
the step, the sun evaporates
more each hour. I'm sitting

in the gray underwear-colored
sky listening to Tyrone Davis
and Marianne Faithfull. Yeah,

I'm bleak, but here are two
gazanias who haven't buckled
under to winter's government.

One is orange, the other's purple.
Frost wraps frozen hands around
their stems. Each night they

wriggle free. Hail, plucky
gazanias who do not bend
to the calendar's back pages.

Hail to you, desert flowers
who swing open orange and purple
gates for us to walk through.

URGENCY OF ASTILBE

I knew Joanne and I
were going to be friends
when she said that she too
watches Rhineland astilbe
light the blackest night
with pink star plumes--
astilbe blooms
up a storm, and there you are,
scared, looking behind you,
but instead of fear
you see a pink messenger
bringing you a letter
from gods and goddesses
just writing to find out
how you are
and signing their names
in hot pink ink.

ORANGE MIMULAS

So close to the soil,
you can miss her,
but an orange mimulus
is writing you about
how the wind wants to
blow in your ear. Will
you go and meet
the wind later? Will you
take on faith what
an orange mimulus says
to you, a stranger?

PEAS

With peas, you can have
an almost perfect world.

Build a trellis.
Green monkeys,
they climb it.

White blossoms, Magellan
circling the globe.

Pick them. Put them
in a basket. Take them
to the sink. They enter
the water,

otters now, slipping
past your fingers.

SWEET PEA

I start my sweet
peas downstairs, give
them tube lighting,
good potting mix,

water, put them
under a baggie. What
a way to begin life!

They poke up,
get big enough to make
love to a fence. How
they curl and bloom. *Oh,*

sweet pea, come on
and dance with me
sang Tommy Roe in '66.
They are dancing

with me. Hey,
they're even dancing
with dew, the sun's
gold medallion on
the sky's cloud chest.

BUTTERCUPS

Not yellow like the sun,
a burping star
some 90 million miles away,
buttercups are yellow screams,
yellow accidents right before
my eyes. When a buttercup

opens her yellow door,
I come on in and plop down
on her best yellow chair.
In a buttercup's yellow house,
I wear nothing. I'm usually pale,
but my skin looks so

yellow in here I think wow,
I'm just about ready to pop
right open. Buttercups
turning and turning even
deeper yellow by the day,
a carousel for bees.

TEXAS BLUEBONNETS

I start them downstairs
in early March.
Four blip up,
and one of those dies.
But three thrive,
tiny blue blossoms.
In Pennsylvania
a Texas sky
blue floating before
the red
and yellow of a desert
peace rose.

COREOPSIS INTELLIGENCE

In a stuffed room
someone yammers on
about a new volume

she's co-editing,
calls it *killing* work.
Another says he's presenting
a paper in Albuquerque
which will *put all other*

Faulknerians out of business.
Everyone agrees that
everyone here is brilliant.
They have the paperwork
and gilded syllables

to prove it. How I long
to get free and slip
into the captivity of my garden, yellow
coreopsis, 20 suns rising

by my leg--not any
ordinary yellow, but
a brilliant yellow that
makes others look paltry
pale--with nothing

to prove. One bloom
puts them miles ahead of
anyone in the room.

HOLLYHOCK BUDS

open, deep crimson
first catching fire
from the bottom
up. Flame heads

to the northernmost
tip: flowers
leaping back and

forth to the moon,
birds awking and flying
quickly away,
firestalk burning

throughout July and clear
into August.

FERNS HAVE

Ferns have a lot of nerve
sprawling over your feet,
brushing your calves,
but they bend green

bodies away, toward the pond,
tell you they're promised
to the wind.

In spring, ferns go
spiraling up, tapping winter
on the shoulder and saying,
"You'll have to go now."
Winter obeys. Then the woods
become their inheritance.

Autumn turns each
frond brown.
They look up at leaves
in falling sunlight—
betrayed, breaking at the edges,
shredding themselves like paper.

FERN HARRY

By his back step,
a lacy green
trampoline of fern
fronds.   It's true

that ferns do little
except bounce
a bit in a breeze.
They like a sedentary

life, couch potatoes
of forest or garden.
Harry likes their
triangular shadow,

the world not a circle
or a square, but a
flittery shape.
In his dark green shirt,

Harry dangles his feet
on the top of his ferns,
summer sky a gray
box breaking up.

PURPLE LOOSESTRIFE

My purple loosestrife
stands beside a bee balm.

Bees indeed see
its blossoms as balm,
sample each, lavender
bleeding through
wings. They look like
little psychedelic pilots.

Not the purple loosestrife,
with lavender lining
thin branches. I run
past it to strawflowers
and phlox. When I see
that the lavender
has gone, I pass the bee
balm heading indoors,

a driver on a highway
who finds the one road
she needs just closed.

DEADHEADING

Mother would put ten peas
on my plate. I swallowed them
with milk, ten green aspirins. Then

I could go. I was raised
to be "well balanced," a lame goal,
meant to keep malls moving and

bankers bopping. I've never met
a well balanced person who didn't
fret about too tall grass. Now

I'm the daddy of petunias,
all healthy, my pride and joys. I'd
love to find a bumpersticker

that says: **I'm the Proud Father
of a Folsom Avenue Honors Petunia.**
For their own good, I deadhead

each one each morning to make
them blossom more. Pulling off
what's dead keeps them from

going to seed. A barbarism,
this family value, but I go on,
picking, discarding.

QUIVER OF ROSE

I'm not sure how
many studies have been done, how
many polls taken, how
many surveys sent, but I doubt
most lovers discuss April
Stevens and Nino Tempo's
Atco 45s
after sex, doubt
most prefer Popsicles to red
delicious apples, and I doubt
most lovers watch Dobie Gillis
in the tender twilight though
your spiritual resemblance
to Zelda Gilroy and mine to
Maynard G. Krebs scares me, and
if the so-
ciologist,
pollster, or
survey taker
comes to the door
I will tell the sociologist,
pollster or survey taker
they can't send the Grand
Canyon's sunset through
a scanner, can't pull orchids
from a #2 pencil, and can't
tabulate the quiver
of rose petals in light rain.

YOU CAN GO WHERE THE ROSES GO

Before a rose dies, she pays each bill
in the Bank of Trees, makes out her will
with a Lawyer of Bees, and sees
Death sees her looking away. Red blossoms,

a rose spends her life writing an operating
manual for pebbles--how to bask in light
when you're stationed under roots. Red blossoms,
a job well

done--who knows? I may not be here very long,
so I should read that manual too. Then I can
go where the roses go in winter's snowy
music: Death and her roots reminisce about

red blossoms.

VENUS FLYTRAP

Mine grows in a red plastic
cup, sphagnum moss
surrounding it with a yearning
for a swamp it never knew.

Green traps open
under a transparent dome,
hoping for food, flesh
landing like a dream.

But flies are safe. Ants
pace around the sill.
Sunlight slides on
a yellow sift of sand.

Still, the mean thing ups
and invents new shoots.
Through its cage, stars
enter, triggering a trap.

SOME FIERCE BEGONIAS

The phone rings as I'm putting
on my running clothes.
Miss Terri, our secretary, asks
if she should pick up my plane
tickets in the business office.
Yes, I say if it's not too much
trouble. The day goes on that way,
they all do, unless a sick cat
undoes me or I read a KKK
candidate is heading for the
statehouse--and then where?
I think of you and how you're
chicory in my coffee
even though you live in Florida.
I want one bed to stretch
1000 miles, step outside and see
some fierce begonias.
Late October. Waxy pink petals
test a cold thermometer.
They don't give in. I run
and run and run, my body
a stem straining with buds.

BEES ON A SUNFLOWER

Vicki hates bees but likes watching
how they relish a sunflower,
the sun balanced between each wing.

If bees could be bees and not sting,
she'd visit them hour after hour.
Vicki hates bees but likes watching

these trapeze artists in full swing,
summer at its highest power,
the sun balanced between each wing.

She often spends half the morning
by stalks unless there's a shower.
Vicki hates bees but likes watching

gold blossoms vibrate with buzzing,
each stem a tall honey tower,
the sun balanced between each wing—

time turns flowers into nothing
but empty fields cold winds devour.
Vicki hates bees but likes watching
the sun balanced between each wing.

SQUIRREL AND SUNFLOWER

Look, you gray-tailed acrobat
    jumping from phone wire
to branch, I have a bone to pick.
    If not a bone, then a blossom
    to pick with you, except
that you've already picked it.

My sunflower. I planted the seed
in April, but here in late August
    you think it's a strange yellow
planet you can topple. Even

    that's not enough--you've got to eat
    it whole. You're no squirrel--
    you're a cat burglar,
    a spy, a petal swindler.

When I step outside in the morning,
    the green stalk's all bent over.
    This must not be
a world made for flowers--this world's
    made for teeth. Go, squirrel,
    are you ready to inform the bee?

NICOTIANA

On opposing sides
of the picnic table
we drink iced tea. How
very Illinois: bees bounce
up from window wells, cars
gossip in driveways,
a prairie wind fondles
weeds. Scent of nicotiana
overtakes us. I swear

you have the sun under
your nails and it smells
like these flowers. No sun,
you say. I'm drowsy,
though I've done nothing
all day, the garden hose
a green penis watering
the lawn. You, a man
from an airline ad claiming

your service is tops,
your skies friendly.
Not mine. Thunder walks them,
and soon rain will fall on
the nicotiana, morning
starting its long walk
to bring clouds umbrellas.

LATE AUGUST GARDEN

Bees travel blue salvia
and yellow rudbeckia,
a canna's orange-red
lighthouse beam spotting
dark earth. I'm

welcomed twice—
first by the garden,
then by Jean and Phil.

Work
in a garden is also
escape from work—
the constant feeding
and watering
where months are years.
In August, I doubt

December, yet that bit
of withered grass
beside tall, white nikkis—

ice sleeps in the most
profuse flowering. To think

of so many plants coming
in for the winter,
spring's distant bells
drowned out by snow-spray.
They show me bamboo

almost ten feet tall. Phil
says the green dies
within minutes
of getting cut. No one
can hold onto it. You
let it go—

like this garden, still
giving, still open. Already
fading away.

AUGUST SWEET PEAS

I'm having unclean
thoughts about my sweet pea,
wondering if some night
I'll go out and snip it down

or at least pare it back. Out
of control, it's buried the ageratum,
dwarfed the balsam,
this party crasher who drinks

all my best liquor, passes out
on my floor. Yes, in March
I was thrilled when he started
gaining green, still thrilled

when buds began to form
in May. In June the vine
went outrageously mad, blooming
its green head off, but now

my other plants bristle.
Even the fence is tired
of holding it up. But I won't go
out and slit its throat, will let

its fireworks fizzle
as they are now, in August,
traces of yellow on a green river,
an autumn twinge in its roots.

III. LETTING GO

H.D., THE RAIN, AND THE PEAR TREE

She was always sewing together
the torn sleeves of extremes.
One summer her friend Bill Williams
saw her in a field waiting for rain.
"Come, beautiful rain," she said,
again and again. Clouds funneled
into her skin. Wet hair blotted out
her slack face. Her clothes held her
up like a boat on a lake.
She looked so beautiful, not the way
mountains do or dusk's red hammock;
hers was wilder: trapezoids leaping
free of their sharp shapes.

Another time, she was struck
by a pear tree. The silver leaves
were so ordinary, so completely usual,
a passerby could miss how easily
their shine darkened the orchard,
put evening into the tip
of a firefly. No scissors of heat
could cut them off the tree
for no fire was hotter than these.
Even in winter when the branches
were a shambles of cold wet cotton,
the memory of each leaf stoked
a fire in the roots.

Her poem became the odor of fruit
remembered as a childhood dream.
It was that frightening, but even
more luscious.

10:55 MAPLE

I'm catching
the 10:55 maple

to the sky- -
it's never late

or on time,
just is. Leaves

click down
a track of clouds,

bounce but make
no sound. When I

get to the sky,
I don't know my

final destination.
Heaven? Please,

no gold streets,
no fancy places

underling angels
must wash. Maybe

I'd do better
without any arrival

time, no schedule,
just ride

this tree
to the end

of the line
which has no end.

MAPLE, 3:18 P.M.

I've lived in places without
a tree, only a window
with a street view. Even
desert monks who holed
up in caves could go out
for a tree's eye view of

this life. Cars and
sidewalks give a sadness
that crawls down the eyes
and up the spine. To this
maple, I'm just another
squirrel, whether I rake
what it drops or not. Wind

falls and sun madcaps
through leaves. I wait
for a storm, purple
clouds welting over branches.

A TREE CALLS YOU

but you're unlisted. Your life's
misfiled, mislaid, mis-
taken. Tonight a tree calls

you, not long distance -- just
open your window. Fireflies
doze in a leaf
hammock before lighting
a field, the electric company
in mid-air. A tree calls

you names birds call you in
secret. You don't answer. Careful,
would you want a tree to think
you rude? Don't worry.
Trees don't snub. They shade.
Listen,

her still voice again -- the tree,
her taproot belly laugh.
Branches offer you a hand.

BATHING TREES

Some people lack green
Thumbs -- their bodies
and minds are greener
than any hill, any park --
so naturally birds, flowers,
and animals thrive

around them. Ancient
rumor has it that St. Francis
could call birds
and they'd come -- even if
they were busy performing
in some sky circus.

Was God the green
within him? When I call birds
they whiten me. My hibiscus
is right this minute
on life support. I'm told
I have a green thumb --

That's the problem. A thumb
isn't deep enough to bloom
a spirit. I watch trees
bathing in photosynthesis,
stretch out my arms,
hope.

DARK LINE

the dark
line
of trees
thins   and
dis

appears   dawn
on leaf
tips

un
folds
darts
a hollow
pink
tongue

to my roof's
rain
gutters

CRAB APPLE DYING

Well done, sweet tree,
who gave summers of buds
breaking into blossoms
breaking into bees. Your
apples reminded us of solar
systems jam packed
with planets so red
we wondered do gods and

goddesses eat planets when
they're hungry? Now
your top branches know only
winter, we can see through
the middle, and only
a few leaves struggle
to green. The owner says
you must come down--an empty

space where apples hung
and late August air smelled
like wine. Go, tree,
although you may find
no heaven, clasp our small
thanks to your trunk.
It's your time.
Ours is coming.

SEPTEMBER BOUGAINVILLEA

September is
falling leaves of notebook
paper while violet
bougainvillea moons
rise over roofs
of petunias and asters,
moons that only the first
frost can make set.

SEPTEMBER ASTERS

Waiting is not all,
but it helps if you love
asters. Not patient,
I want everything

done five minutes ago,
want a day to hurry up
and get done before 24 hours,
want a year to be 234 days

instead of 365. With asters,
I learn patience,
dailiness. Come August,
tiny buds show up. It's not

like they're in any hurry
to open. They amble
toward September, swelling
a little each day. A few

finally open, blue
boats heading into a lake of light.
Then it's the whole plant.
Sailing.

CELESTE ASTERS

They're purplish turtles
sticking bloomheads
out to get sun. Autumn
withdraws leaves from

the First National Bank
of Maples as Celeste
asters send purplish
signals deep into the sky.
They're utterly, utterly
nude. It's true,

the moon leers at them,
but they carry on
even under pinpricks
of rain.

MADWOMAN IN THE GARDEN

I wait for rain. Here
the sky is too clear.
The mayor says to stop sprinkling,
but I don't listen. Buckets out back,
I give poppies their one joy.
I dislike our mayor anyway- -
I am better off between portulacas
and white roofs of candytuft.

I don't get out much. Used to
attend the United Methodist Church
but they only loved me
for committees I could serve on.
Dorcas Circle ladies still call
but I bore them with balsam
and they hang up.

Someday they'll find me, burst
woman, hoe-in-hand. Body a mulch
basket before the grapevine.
They can prop me up
against their fear
for my soul, and let me go.
My garden is deep.
I'll find my way back.
One spring,
the wettest in decades,
the new owners of my house will say:
whoever lived here before
was a genius-in-bud.
In forming grapes

trailing through tendrils,
I will be there, listening.

WAITING ROOM NASTURTIUMS

In the doctor's
waiting room, our

nervous faces.
Some can't hide
what ails them --
a cough, a sneeze.
Others wait while
sickness works
under their coats,
their skin.

A woman pulls out
a chocolate kiss
from her purse,
unwraps and eats it,
then goes for another.
I see her face,

relaxed,
her eyes
like calm places
full of nasturtiums.

ELEGY WITH CUCUMBER BLOSSOMS

I had that dream
again: I wake up not knowing
where I am -- Tennessee?
Wisconsin? Pennsylvania?
No. I'm in Myrt's house
and she puts cake on the table.
Half deaf, she smiles
with eighty years in one
place underlining her lips.

My eyes open. I know
she is dead -- she melts
like ice on the window.
An early frost on
the cucumber's yellow blossoms
snatches the fruit
from a dawn-torn blanket:

blackened leaves cover
what cannot be assumed
about this year's harvest.

CHRYSANTHEMUM

The mailman sun
delivers nothing.
Your petals need
news. Empty,
empty, you can't
hold on much longer.
Leaves and green
gone, you stand
alone, woman
in a red hat
at a jaunty angle,
waiting.

CHRYSANTHEMUM CHALK

If I could write
something 100 times,
what would it be?

Had I been
chalk
and not a flower,
would I spend my days
waiting to be
used? People with

scissors come at me.
I am something
to cut,
part of an arrangement.
I separate
talkers at a table.
Had I been chalk

in a human hand,
I'd vanish,
move closer
to erasure,
but still leave
many messages,

brief ones
before disappearing,
a November
blossom.

CODE BLUE ABUTILON

You dug it up in October,
handed it to me,
said please take care

of it over winter,
that your house has
bad light. So I care

for this abutilon
which shines red
searchlights through

the shades. How happy
she is! Almost happy
as winter forming

in a gray sky,
claws out. Now
the red searchlights

turn off, green
leaves yellow and
fall. It may be days,

weeks at best. Or
will spring come
just in time

to get it outside
again -- or back to
your house with good

light on the side
where it grew
dusk by a back step.

NOVEMBER PARSLEY

I don't trust my lover,
so easy with compliments,
too quick to adore.
And I am tired of going
to malls, envying mannequins
their poise and pliability.

So I go into the garden
for parsley sprigs:
green as they were in June,
filling me with hope,
an acrid belief.

Roses have already given
themselves to winter.
Both sunflowers long ago
fattened the squirrels,
but this parsley
buckling the hard earth --

my veins brim over
with their tenacious tunes.

DECEMBER STRAWFLOWERS

Many frosts dagger
the garden, yet these
won't call it a day,
a week,
or even a season--

one strawflower
blooms orange under
winter's freezing flame,
orange like sun buttons
sewn on summer's

shroud. In July
I overlooked them.
Now they tap orange
scepters on noggins
of falling temperatures.

ORCHIDS IN ANTARCTICA

When they release the movie of June
Cleaver ripped by osprey in Madagascar,
millions come. Many leaders talk

about family values in pressed trousers
and good haircuts. Their children look
like them, lonely.

I am my family -- I live alone.
Well, I do have two cats,
but the census didn't record them.
I keep a roof over my head while
my soul sleeps downstairs. The family's
an orchid

in Antarctica -- love the petals, marvel
at its tenacity, and wear snowshoes
trying to track its bud.

WINDOWBOX IN WINTER

This one lies on four feet
    of red brick.
  I remember the man who fixed it
so carefully last June,
   a green hose wrapping him
like a python loose in the suburbs.
  To see the brown stalks
in the brown box
 denies all I smelled months ago.
Sunlight
   makes them stand out: hideous
 and too quiet. Still, they stand
not bending
  with snow or rain or wind.
 I would like to think of them
as dignified
  but for the rot.
Maybe because of the rot.

ORDERING

In early winter, seed
catalogues introduce me

to swingin'-for-the-fences
roses, glads that never look
preached-at or solemn. Even
the ordering sheet gives
a thrill, lines I can fill
with promises of bloomburst --

searching these pages
is like when I'm cold so
I sink into a hot bath,
the steamy room
like a greenhouse
with orchids. While
winter eats its roast ice
sandwich, ink stains me

like marigolds,
strong stems of possibilities.

Kenneth Pobo was born in 1954 and grew up in Villa Park, Illinois. His interest in gardening began when he was a child; he began writing poetry in 1970, imitating songs such as "Crystal Blue Persuasion." His eclectic garden continues to inspire many of his poems. He teaches English at Widener University. Among his interests, besides gardening and poetry, are collecting obscure records from the 1960s, film, concern for the environment and human rights issues. He shares his life with his partner Stan and two cats, Preston and Margot.

Mr. Pobo's published books/chapbooks are:

Open To All, 2River Press, online chapbook, 2000
Cicadas and Apple Trees, Palanquin Press, 1998
       (Winner of a 1998 Palanquin Poetry Award)
A Barbaric Yawp On the Rocks, Alpha Beat Press, 1997
Ravens and Bad Bananas, Osric Press, 1996
Ferns On Fire, Nightshade Press, 1992
Yes: Irises, Singular Speech Press, 1991
Evergreen, Bragdon Press, 1985
A Pause Inside Dusk, Song Press, 1984
Billions of Lit Cigarettes, Raw Dog Press, 1981
Musings From The Porchlit Sea, Branden Press, 1979

"In its deceptive simplicity of language and tone -- its implicit serenity -- Ken Pobo's poetry bears a family resemblance to Oriental nature poetry. Like the best haiku, too, his poems are full of a passive wisdom and a wonder about the world, floating on deep philosophical waters. The poems in ORDERING: A SEASON IN MY GARDEN are a delight to read for the peace they evince, the facility with language they demonstrate."

-- Charles Rammelkamp.

Cover photograph by JamieCollins Photography, Glastonbury, Connecticut.